Black Threads

Books by Jeff Friedman

The Record-Breaking Heat Wave
Scattering the Ashes
Taking Down the Angel
Black Threads

Black Threads

Jeff Friedman

Carnegie Mellon University Press
Pittsburgh 2007

Acknowledgments

My thanks to the editors of the following publications in which these poems first appeared:
Ars-Interpres ("Taking the South" and "Out of Reach"); *The Alembic* ("Salt House" and "The Twist"); *Bloomsbury Review* ("Mournful Dress"); *Crab Orchard Review* ("In the Hospital"); *Cutthroat* ("Hymn to Your Tongue"); *Five AM* ("Songs," "Night of the Rabbi" and "Sunday School"); *Forward* ("Memorial"); *Home Planet News* ("My Mother Tells Me about Her Father"); *Hunger Mountain* ("Folding Fan"); *Judaism* ("Two Women"); *The Louisville Review* ("After the Storm" and "Goodbye"); *Luna* ("Nuevo Laredo" and "The Surviving Angel"); *Maggid* ("Lineage" and "Sunday"); *Mystic River Review* ("Window"); *Natural Bridge* ("Dinner at the Warwick," "Buying Another Year," "Lament," "Cain and Abel," and "Call from Little Rock"); *The New Republic* ("Punishment"); *Nightsun* ("Video Games" and "Crows"); *Poet Lore* ("Hanging Sculpture"); *Poetry East* ("Birthday"); *Prairie Schooner* ("The Promised Land" and "Jacob and the Angel"); *Rattle* ("Watching the Bat"); *River Styx* ("The Golem in the Suburbs"); *The Saint Ann's Review* ("The Long Heat Wave"); *Tarpaulin Sky* ("Stockboy"); *Tar River Poetry* ("Night of the Bat" and "Making It to Tina Turner").

"The Long Heat Wave" was printed as a limited edition letterpress broadside in 2005 by The Center for Book Arts in New York City. "The Long Heat Wave" was also reprinted in the fifth anniversary issue of *The Saint Ann's Review*. "Memorial" was reprinted in the *The Other Side of Sorrow*. "Late Shift, Minneapolis Welding Rod" was recently published by *The American Democracy Project*, April 5, 2006 (http://ee.iusb.edu/index.php?/adp/blog/national_poetry_month_jeff_friedman/).

I am grateful to the New Hampshire State Council on the Arts for a grant that helped me to complete this collection.

My thanks to Colleen Randall, Ken Smith, Christopher Noel, Roy Nathanson, Charna Meyers, Ross Gay, Steven Schreiner and Chard deNiord for their help, insight and encouragement. A special thanks to Howard Schwartz, Sharon Dolin and Judith Vollmer for their close attention to the whole collection of poems.

Book design: Rubén F. Quintero

The publication of this book is supported by a grant from the Pennsylvania Council on the Arts.

PENNSYLVANIA
COUNCIL
ON THE
ARTS

40th Anniversary

Contents

FOUR

for Colleen

There are no stars tonight
But those of memory.
Yet how much room for memory there is
In the loose girdle of soft rain.

—Hart Crane

ONE

The Golem in the Suburbs

Everything will be okay,
my father said, but he lied,
then plotted to kill me. He raised me
from the dust, from four letters
of the alphabet repeated in the right

sequence seven times,
from the secret names of God.
He was the last to go.
I squeezed the air from his windpipe
and threw him down, a breathless heap.

Now my killing binges have ended.
My skin turns blue.
I stumble through the suburbs, looking
for someone I can talk to, but no one
comes out of the silent wood houses.

The magic tablet melts
under my tongue. Flies thicken,
a loud humming in their dark brains.
Read the word on my forehead,
Truth or *Death?*

The Surviving Angel

After the war shredded his wings
and brought him down to earth, limping,

after the flames ravaged the hills,
and the seizures stopped and disease scarred his face,

after the windows shattered,
after the charred fields and the smoking plain,

after the unforgettable screams of his friends,
the lost opportunities, the nights of forgetting,

after the bleak sun broke the horizon once more,
he found a home among those who didn't know

his language, didn't know
he was an angel. He would speak their language

in the streets or in the stores, but only
with great effort, and he knew they mocked him

when he walked away. Each afternoon
as he worked in the garden, planting

new flowers and tending vegetables,
he squeezed the black dirt and rubbed it

on cheeks and forehead, then pushed
his hands deeper into the earth.

Now he remembered
the sound of striped bees hitting the windows

and the great sighs of angels
stretching their long, feathery limbs after love.

Mournful Dress

As the room tilted,
the piano played on
and the mournful dress,

caught in the wind,
swirled over the crushed
white orchids.

Wings laden
with cargoes of oil
lifted over our heavy

tired lids.
Air dusted us
with a dark pollen.

Across avenues of smoke
black wingtips clacked—
kicked the clocks

cawing at their feet.
And the pillars of our future
toppled on the cracked

gleaming staircase
though our families lingered
like pungent scents.

Still, as the piano
groaned at dusk,
and the mournful dress

swirled under a rainbow
that would soon be snuffed
by the sooty sky,

we leaned toward
each other for a last
pearly kiss.

Driving through the Rubble

All over Reseda
power lines were down,
shop windows shattered.

The black streets glittered.
As we drove through the rubble,
we heard on the car radio

that the looting had started,
that the river had broken
through the dam.

I saw a man
kicking another man
who curled into a ball

and tried to roll
away. "Don't look,"
you said. Sirens

flashed everywhere,
alarms sounded.
On the underground

station, the refrain
"It's nature's way of telling you . . ."
played over and over

while somewhere on the Boulevard
birds picked up
their voices and took off

for Mexico. I touched
your bare knee,
"It'll be okay."

For hours,
anxious to get away,
we sped down the highway—

the speed-limit signs
ticking in our wake,
miles of asphalt

spreading out before us
like a blank space in the mind,
waiting for memory.

At the Barstow exit
we stopped
at a Copper Penny,

where we sat near a window
so we could watch
the cars pull in

to the parking lot.
We had just enough
money to order Penny Specials

and ate slowly,
pretending to enjoy
the greasy burgers and fries.

An orange light
bathed your cheeks
and forehead. I wondered

how much damage
had been done. "Should we
go home?" I asked.

"Not yet." When we got
back on the highway
a lone hawk

took off from the high
boulders and stroked
its spotted wings

against still air
and you shuddered—
then it swooped

down over us, diving
for a field mouse
or snake coiled

in dry brush.
Iridescent blue clouds
bulked over the mountains,

and the horizon leaned
toward us. The day
was shutting down.

Where the highway ended,
we took the last exit,
300 miles from home.

Lineage

My mother's people came from St. Louis—
before that, from Galicia,

but my father had no people.
He came from a silent village drifting in ash.

He came from an empty barn.
He came from a nest of blue eggs,

from a hillside of tired cows, from a yard
where chickens scratched out a living.

He dreamed a family of crows.
He dreamed a sky full of roads,

a wedding in the pines,
his pockets stuffed with twenties.

He dreamed a gray silk suit,
black wingtips whose polish wouldn't scuff,

a brown fedora bobbing in the blue light,
a new set of hard luggage.

He dreamed a Cadillac with bright wings,
the bugles that would announce his arrival.

He dreamed a red highway.
He dreamed his last breath.

He called himself a bad penny,
smoke in a blind eye.

He dreamed a sales pitch
that would never fail.

Folding Fan

When I unfold the fan, breeze turns
to warm wind, jangling silver
chimes. A red bird skitters in flight
and a wooden fence stretches
toward the horizon, where the sky blushes.
Under the sycamores gnats swarm the gray
blocks of sidewalk, and blue butterflies
cluster juniper heads, wings spread.
I run my stick over the wooden slats
just to hear the clatter. Across the street
some little girl bounces her round ball
on the pavement harder and harder until it
hangs in the air above her like a giant red apple.
In our apartment my sister curtsies and dances
the flamenco, wide red skirt flaring
as her heels punish the linoleum, scuffed
with black marks. My mother oils
the cherry hardwood table, rubs it with a cloth.
Now my uncle, shirt sleeves rolled up to his elbows,
brown forehead shining through his thinning hair,
walks down the block holding his fiancée's hand.
He leans toward this tall, thin woman with a pasty face,
his fleshy lips pursed. For a moment everything
holds still—my mother at the window,
my sister with her leg cocked,
ready to stomp down on the floor,
my uncle's lips puckered against the air,
the silver chimes hooked above the window,
long tubes glinting—and then
my father arrives—suit rustling—
swift as a mailman and noisy as traffic,
with gifts for everyone and crumpled
dollar bills dropping out of his pockets.

Buying Another Year

for Gerald Auten

Our broom bristles
rip up
pieces of asphalt,
leaving the gray
rippled surface
in patches. Where
water pools,
we soak it up
with rags, then wait
for sun to dry
the wet spots.
"I coated my father's
roof," Jerry says,
"almost every summer."
Lean and sinewy,
he rests on the broom
handle a moment,
his face red
from working in the sun.
"We worked on it
together, but now
he's too old
to go up a ladder."

We dip our brushes
in the bucket
and spread the tarry
asphalt. He lets
his brush glide
over the roof as if painting
a smooth wall.
I try to imitate him,
but soon I bend over
pressing on the handle,
and my back aches.
"It's easy—just go with it."
In places where the roof
bubbles and blisters,
I push down harder,

brushing back and forth
and across.
I squiggle the brush
bristles in the craters
that surround the nails.

In the distance leaves
are starting to turn
and shadows drop
from the pines.
I see the rotting
wood under the eaves
and the spots where paint
has chipped off
the fascia. "This coating'll
buy you another year,"
he says, but nothing's
for sure, and a wind
rushing through the pines
rains down long
green needles
on the gleaming tar.

Night of the Rabbi

"No son of mine is quitting
Hebrew school," my father declares,
pounds his fist on the table.
Judah trembles in the South
and glittery forks twirl
in air like 5-pointed stars,
and the rabbi closes his eyes
as he rocks in the squeaky chair.

While my sisters bow their heads
to their plates and the rabbi says a blessing
over the brisket, ruddy and tender,
my mother touches her index
finger to the spot between her eyes,
signaling I should adjust my glasses.
The windows steam up as the rabbi
raises his knife toward the ceiling
like Abraham hunching over his son.
"Where's the lamb?" I ask.

He chews and talks,
telling the story about the rabbi
who lost his sidelocks in Vegas,
the rabbi who forgot to kiss
the mezuzah and couldn't get a congregation
for five years, the rabbi
and the funeral of the Jewish hit man,
"The nicest guy on earth."
A light spreads over the table
as he recalls a thousand bar mitzvahs,
fortunes made in gifts,
and I imagine a room full of pen
and pencil sets, monogrammed
handkerchiefs, and tie clips.

Now the rabbi rasps
Yiddish folk songs,
clapping his hands and laughing.
"He gets a free meal
every night," I blurt out,
but my sisters sing along
and my father's face falls,
his snoring loud as a plague
of locusts, and my mother lights
a candle in the burning bush.

Blessing for the Hats

Say a blessing for the hats
that waltz over the hard floors,
that bob on the ocean of their own

making with their memories intact.
Say a blessing for the sweaters
that gave too much of themselves,

clinging relentlessly, that unraveled
or stretched until their fibers
snapped. Say a blessing

for the fossils humming in your nails
and teeth, for the kisses that remember
your lips. Say a blessing for

the bones that gave in to love,
putting on their bodies and walking out
at daybreak. Say a blessing for the

body with its narrow caves,
for the clattering cups, the noisy
prayers, for the heat of the eyes,

the wild burning, the sweet
smell of flesh, the rain
ripping up the rusty river.

Noah Looks Back

I remember the flood, the river
of ashes, the crushed stones,
the glinting ores. Families
vanished in a flash, but the cries
continued for centuries, oblivious
waves of sound shattering
against teeth. I remember the shells
whispering, the doves flying
out at dawn into the lush
foliage. The ark shipwrecked
on the tip of God's tongue.
I remember the unending vowels
echoing in the dark, the salt
crusted on my lips. Fish
swam in white sand.
Promises rained from the sky
into thorny beds
where lovers were knotted.

I remember the dense effluvia,
the faint ribs, the indistinct
lines, the hanging genitals
disappearing into rock, the lost
eons calling from the caves,
calling through brittle bones
blasted with gamma rays,
the black candles on the shore,
prophets buried in sand—
the carnage quiet
on their swollen blue lips.

Miriam

Come to me under the sticky clouds
where light hangs on thorns
and darkness spreads over our lips.

Come to me with your glittering forks,
your swollen gourds, your baleful
eyes and hungry horizon.

Come to me with your ten plagues
cloaked in the towering cloud,
twisting over our shattered ground,
over bodies strewn in ditches.

Come to me with torn silks,
burning hat, silvery
heels, your bangles tinkling like threats,
echoes eating through bone.

Let raptors feast, tearing
out the entrails of rotting corpses.
Let the voice walking in the garden
rip off the taut skin
of its drum. Let your black
flower open its jaws.

Let me touch your bruised skin,
and taste your wounds—
come to me, my sea of bitterness,
my Miriam.

Birthday

Time was flowing
in the middle of the night, and a silk
scarf floated down on me.

Your blue dress tensed
on its hanger, waiting
to go out. The heels

of your shoes clicked
against each other
and made a wish.

In the middle of the night
my hands drew
your shape in the air.

My arms waltzed with your shadow.
In the middle of the night
the stars glistened,

and your lips grew dewy.
The smell of honeysuckle
lingered in your hair.

In the middle of the night
I set the cake on the table, sugary
and bright, but nothing

waited at the back
of your breath to
blow out the candles.

TWO

My Mother Tells Me about Her Father

He died so long ago
he's only a shadow
in the corner of a room,

his face lit by a reading lamp,
peering into the Talmud.
I barely knew him.

Sometimes I see his fingers
slide over a piece
of cloth. Sometimes

I feel them grazing my skin
as he pulls his yellow tape
measure from my waist to my ankle.

I hear his breathing,
the whistle in his lungs
when he speaks.

What else is there to tell?
He was small and thin,
the same height as my mother.

He had very thin ankles—
like a girl's—and large
beautiful brown eyes.

I don't remember my father ever
kissing me, even on the cheek.
At the service I stared

at the rabbi's black beard
and listened to the mournful chanting
but never shed a tear.

After he died, my mother
went to work in a garment factory
pulling threads.

I remember how she sat
by herself in the kitchen,
how her hands trembled.

She had such beautiful hands,
and her face looked so sad and worried.
That's when I cried.

In the Hospital

When my mother opens her eyes,
she's at the 1904 World's Fair,
eating an ice cream cone for the first time, pressing
her left hand into her mother's palm,
an immense heat breathing into the park.

Vanilla ice cream melts down her chin
onto fingers she licks one by one.
She and her mother saunter past show tents
pegged into soft, damp ground,
past Igorots sprawled in dried grass,
bodies gleaming like polished leather,
spears flung down like broken sticks,
past glistening ores, columns of bees,
past the ark on Mount Ararat
and the cage that holds the last unicorn.

Mosquitoes hatch in standing water
and swarm over the crowd. Her mother swats
them, but she can't stop the mosquitoes
from biting. She can't stop the typhoid *bacillus*
from spreading through her daughter's blood.
Now she sits at bedside,
singing lullabies and telling stories,
massaging her daughter's face and chest with cold cloths.

When my mother opens her eyes, breath gathers
in the tube plugged into her throat
and the digital readout blinks red in the dark.
Pumps sigh, and the nurse's cart
clatters over the vinyl floor.

When she opens her eyes, speckled blackbirds
wake in the crevices of old buildings.
The air rests on her soft, still cheeks.
When she opens her eyes, hope
rains from the sky. The ark rises
onto dry land. Shadows of doves
fly out at dawn into the cool light.

Songs

For the school talent show, my sister
practices "Getting to Know You"
in the living room, her voice cracking
across the words "You're my cup of tea."

I close the door to my bedroom and stare
at the misshapen map she has painted by numbers
on my wall, Missouri in burnt umber—
without a boot heel. I lie down on my bed

and wait for the noise to end. Outside
Steve Miltie, a sophomore in high school,
polishes his new navy blue
Chevy Nova and as he glances up

at the windows where Cathy Cowser lives,
a girl with bony legs and long
brunette bangs, he sings, "Mrs. Brown,
You've Got a Lovely Daughter."

"Going back to Houston, Houston,
Houston," my dad croons, alone
in his Buick Le Sabre as he drives home
from the bar at Via's, the smell of Scotch

permeating the air around him.
Drunk and broke, he's run up another
huge tab, buying drinks for his buddies.
In the kitchen, my mother whips butter, milk,

sugar, eggs and flour into a batter
for her twin pound cakes. She strikes a match
and holds it near the hole of the oven
until the flame beats over the coils

and then she shakes out the match. My mother
doesn't sing. Fingers yellow
from the batter, she sits down at the table
and waits for the two pound cakes to rise from

tins into golden mounds and tries to figure out
how she can put away some money
my father won't know about.
I turn on the underground radio station

and hope "A Day in the Life" will come on
or some other song I can listen to.

Dinner at the Warwick

"Come closer, Chief," he says
and the waiter, tall and thin,
in white shirt and black pants,
bends forward. "I want
my prime rib rare—I mean
real rare." The candlelight

flares in my father's face.
Stubble dark and thick
on his strong square jaw,
he slurs his words,
and dots of spit fly
across the white tablecloth.

Without a glance down, he butters
a hard roll, eats it in two bites,
then knocks the butter knife
off the table with a swipe of his hand
as he boasts about his potential earnings for the year.
I look around, but no one is watching, yet.

Now he gulps another
J&B over one rock
and clinks his glass on the table
and holds it up in the air
to signal he wants a refill.
"Put something in it this time,"

he demands, and the drink waiter
smiles and takes away the empty.
My father reaches over and clasps
my hand—"Good to see you, Son"—
and pins it against the tablecloth. "I really
missed you, you know that?"

He bobs his head,
his hand warm and heavy on mine.
Pieces of brown crust cling
to the sleeve of his blue blazer. I nod.
He's drunk,
and we're a long way from dinner.

Stockboy

In the bins I open a box
of nuts and scoop them into my pockets.
I'm learning what work is, earning
a buck an hour at a job
no one wants, blustering down
long corridors, my polished
shoes clacking against linoleum.
Already my t-shirt is damp

with sweat in the 90-degree heat
and the trucks from downtown bearing
their heavy cargoes downshift at
Steak'n'Shake as they turn
the corner and head toward the loading dock.
Already Joe, the foreman, a lifer
at Famous & Barr, calls my name,
"First shipment, Friedman—

where are you?" in his scratchy
unmusical voice. All day,
as I deliver merchandise
to kitchen, clothing, sporting goods,
appliances, I eat sunflower seeds
and spit out the shells, leaving
a trail through the store so anyone
looking for me knows where I've been.

Late Shift, Minneapolis Welding Rod

for Ken Smith

A white mask strapped
around mouth and nose, Tony
pounds blocks of flux
into particles, packing it in tins.
Flux powders the air
until even the light is white
dust streaming from the fixtures.

Dry, thick and bitter,
the flux coats my tongue,
bakes hard on the rods
moving through the ovens above me.
I scoop up the welding rods
that tumble down the line, slam them
on the metal between tracks,
then fan open my hands
and roll them off my fingertips
into the box sitting on the scale.

I send the box of rods
sliding down the chute's shiny bars
to José, who swigs a jolt
of bourbon from his flask.
He ties the box with wire
and stacks it on the pallet—another
twenty-five pounds
of welding rods to ship
to Northern States Power.

I feel slivers of flux
burning my skin, floating
in my lungs like flakes of rock
in the river or the debris that hangs
in the air after a wrecking ball
buckles the walls of an old warehouse.

Where the cold air that comes in
from the opened door catches it, flux
flies up from the ground in gusts.
And where I lean against the wall
by the unmade boxes, waiting to punch out,
it drifts down from the high
windows like flecks of snow
falling on the midnight floor.

Nuevo Laredo

When I think of Nuevo Laredo
I remember how my friend haggled
a street vendor down
from ten bucks to two bucks
on a switchblade, and walked away happy
until he discovered that, for change,
the vendor had slipped him fake bills.

I remember the blinding heat,
the blue flies that beaded
saloon windows,
the whores sitting on our laps—
"Sucky for tree dolor," they said,
holding up their fingers.

But mostly I remember a small
dirty tent where we watched
a young woman strip
and lie down on a wool blanket.
She made a show of lighting
a cigarette and waving it
as though signaling someone far away.

Then she placed the cigarette between her lips,
took a long, deep drag
and as she opened her legs, jagged
smoke rings puffed out
and we clapped furiously, hoping
to catch her attention.

As we walked past, she buttoned her robe
and put up her thick black
hair, staring through us
as if we were ghosts or weak rays
of light dissipating into the shadows.

I remember the long drive
to the border, the blue coronas
of the moon, the ugly squat
hills, the bats that clung
to trees, the fat bugs
shooting into our beams, the smack
of tires on the rough roads
vibrating through me,
and deep in my chest and throat,
a stunted prayer waiting to
rise like light from water,
like sorrow from dreams, like words
from a fire quenched by dust.

Hanging Sculpture

Made of metal
the bird hangs
from the ceiling
by a wire cable,
tail feathers
flaring. Its one
eye opens
into shadow
and dust.
Bundles of air
bloat its body.

Sometimes the bird
twirls until
the room grows
dizzy, wings
clinging to dappled
migrations through
seven layers
of sunlight. Other
times it is still,
watching for the rainbow
to arc over the
distant hill,
for white doves
to fly out on the waters.

Its voice is a whistle
across silvery bands,
a muttered prophecy
that flowers in the beak,
clenching its dark
kiss of thought.

Watching the Bat

It's the last bat hanging
from the rafters that scares me. Why hasn't
he disappeared like the others
in a spume of smoke at dusk?
Too sick? Too young? Too much of a
loner? I stare at him from my ladder
into the crawl space of the attic,
my flashlight aimed just
below his back. He looks
like a small handful of mud,
tiny bugs breathing inside it.
He looks like a dark mound
in a cemetery or an anthill on asphalt.
He looks like a young boy
in denial about his awful family.
The quivering body holds
the sonar that lets him navigate
the white roads of the moon.
The quivering body holds the
high-pitched song, the quiet
breath that turns blue in
the glass jar of the air.
With my flashlight and my metal
coffee can, I stand on
my ladder into the attic—the pink
feathers of insulation that drift down around me
catching on my sweatshirt and in my hair,
little bits of fiberglass
floating in my lungs—and wait for him
to make a move, but he is no more
than a mouse who clings to the rafters,
a mammal who squeezes his eyes
shut against the light, trying
to get a little sleep.

Palm Reading on Wildwood

"You'll win the lottery!"
The slender young girl
with stringy blond hair ran
her giddy finger over my palm.
"Then you'll stand on a rock overlooking
Angel Falls and make
a wish." With a peanut-butter cookie
in hand, the plump girl
with bright dimples read
Bekka's paw, and my dog let out
a cry that sounded as if it had come
from an exotic rainforest bird.
"She'll live in a mansion and eat
all the biscuits she wants."
Prosperity for both of us—and travel.
The slender girl spun
around and ran down the street
to Sachem Field, where a kite
caught a current of wind
and soared into the sky.
The cute plump girl
watched the yellow streamer
flutter like some kind of dancer.
As she opened her palms,
"Ginny does this all the time,"
my dog stole her cookie
and gulped it down. The girl
ran down the block laughing,
hoping to catch her friend
or find a new one.
And I imagined the kite
soaring above Angel Falls,
where one day I would stand
on a rock and make a wish.
When we got home, my dog
got a biscuit for sitting
and another for lying down
and another for coming when called
and another for staying close to me.

Night of the Bat

The students wear t-shirts, shorts
and sandals, but I'm in jeans and a shirt,
my clothes damp and sticky.
Warm dark air sits
in the open mouth of the windows.
Slowly, meticulously, with a small
piece of yellow chalk,
Megan writes her five-line poem
on the board. After everyone praises it,
I mention that she's shifted tenses
four times in three lines.

"My other teachers say I do that, too."
My eyes sting from sweat
dripping into them. The students float
in a jar of fluorescent air.
Corliss asks again if we can
leave early, but before I can say
no, a black bird plunges
through the windows—a bat
skittering into the light.
"I'm not anxious to get rabies," John says.
Megan corrects him: "Not eager to get rabies."

They scoot their desks back
and toward the door. The bat shoots
toward the window near the video monitor
and lands on the shade, compressing itself
into a mound. Now the students lean
into one another as if riding
a bus that's taken a sharp
turn, and the bat quivers
like a dark ear picking up every
word we say and, like the students,
waiting for me to call it a night.

Video Game

You ride the joystick
until the beam locks in
your target. Then
you press the button
that delivers the payload.

The palaces buckle.
Emerald domes
shatter before they hit
ground, green
stones glinting.

The tents where the poor
live collapse.
Amidst the debris
are the smoking roads.

Orange flames billow
through the countryside.
You can almost feel
the heat under your fingertips.
Colorful balloons burst

like noiseless screams.
You close your eyes
and enter the clouds,
proud of your success,

but your signal breaks up,
and everything turns
to dust, air and rain,
as you hurtle toward a white
wall that won't give.

THREE

The Wedding One Year before the Divorce

Wind plays tricks on the faces
of the bridesmaids, tickling
chubby cheeks, shaking the laughter from them.

My sister, the bride, faints in the arms
of my other sister, who lets her fall into damp grass.
"Give her room to breathe."

"Bet it cost a fortune," my uncle Ernie comments.
"But such a feast," the rabbi answers,
eating the chocolate flowers from a huge hunk of cake.

The sun sprays red light on the party.
The groom rises on a chair, but finds
no one above the crowd and punches the air,

ecstatic, though he already knows
the marriage won't last. Even my Russian
step-grandfather, the sleeve that holds

his stub of arm pinned to his lapel,
dances a little and smiles a lot.
I drink two glasses of wine

and run off to pee on sycamore leaves.
When I return, my father swears he loves everyone
including his boss and his son-in-law,

while my mother swats the flies that swarm the cake,
that rise up like little wizards, weaving
their spell over mourning doves and woozy pigeons.

A little tipsy, I spread my feathers,
tottering on the rim of the rainbow
that arcs over the last wink of wedding.

Window

From the window she sees
the frozen black thread,
clawed shoulders of ice,
the white smash of rock

as she remembers how he mocked her,
mimicking her facial expressions
and voice, the cruel questions
he turned over and over—

always with the pretense
of helping her—until she would
close her eyes and imagine
each question swirling

soundlessly in space like a galaxy
of dead stars. Then she would think of herself
as a target formed in glass
the instant before it flies into

fragments. As she stares at
the snow on the back of the river,
she tries to talk to him,
tries to explain the way she feels

even though she knows he will cut
her off, jump to a subject
that matters little to either of them
and then to another.

Her hands reaching out,
she plummets
into a dark cold river,
and when a ray of light breaks through,

when the silver flames of the torches
light a path to the bottom,
it seems she can almost touch
what she is trying to say.

Lament

For hours I scrubbed the pavement,
but couldn't expunge the shape
of your body chalked in blue.
My fingers traced you

in the dwindling light. I remembered
the shots that took your breath
away, the smell of your life
puddling beneath the curb.

Where was your luck when you needed it?
Where was the cop who patrolled
Jackson Street, circling
the block every five minutes?

Now your sweetness is gone
from the shadows, from the sultry
summer air. And the places
where you walked, where you sat,

where you closed your eyes,
have forgotten you. Smoke hovers
over the green water,
but I see your face

blossoming in the window.
The moths flurry,
the blizzard of their white wings
blurring the speckled dusk.

Punishment

For four thousand years
I've endured the bad metaphors
of self-righteous rabbis who lift

their arms to the sky as if they could
bring on another cataclysm.
I've endured the ridicule of priests,

kings and slaves, the memory
of my husband shepherding our daughters
into the wilderness with his staff. I've endured

fear, the judgment of history
and my own dark thoughts.
Silk robes, spices, urns,

the words of my ancestors—it all burned
to ash, and the ash swirled
in the sea of winds sweeping through the desert.

Great sheets of sand buried
the fire. Cities rose and fell
wickeder than Sodom or Gomorrah.

Each century I gave away
a little more—my index finger,
the tip of my nose, my left breast—

until all that remained was
a broken torso and the unblinking
vision of a bitter memory,

my eyes white and hard
from staring at the same emptiness,
from remembering how comets of fire

hailed down from heaven, torching
the walls of my house. And then
I dissolved into a muffed cry,

into a blinding whiteness,
a few grains of salt
burning the eyes of god.

Jacob and the Angel

after Yehuda Amichai

She balanced on a ledge,
a stony lip
between desire and doubt,

between hope and anger,
her eyes scouring
my face as shadows

wavered at her feet.
"Come," I said.
"It's time to let go

of your fears," but she
flinched, wrapping
her arms around her breasts.

The moon spread
its silky sheet
over white sand.

If she had wings,
they quivered behind her
in the cool night air.

If she had blood
it pulled her downward
toward the restless waves,

toward the earth, waiting
for her return. When
she came to me at last,

the scent of persimmon,
almonds and figs
floated through the night

and a wind passed over my thighs,
and a slow heat rose
through the soles of my feet.

Then I knew her
name and cried out,
falling beneath her.

Cain and Abel

Cain is small
and dark
with knotty muscles,

his skin leathery
from working in the sun,
while his brother is tall

and handsome, a sculpted
face easy to look at
and love.

Abel has a way
with words. When he
closes his eyes

he seems to taste
the prayers in his mouth
like a sweet bread.

Cain doesn't pray—
he talks to God
in the imperative, demanding

His attention. God
rarely listens.
When he does

He hears only belligerence,
greed, a refusal
to accept on faith.

Cain wants equality,
some recognition
of his own worth.

Abel wants more
of everything, more
sheep, more wealth,

more women, a larger
share of the kingdom,
a chance to rule alone.

Cain offers God
the tools he invented
for planting and tilling,

the fruits of his labor—
long rows
of corn and wheat—

but the smell of flesh
roasting in flames
permeates the air.

As Abel sits
on a rock, his brother
falls at his feet,

and the blessing grows
bold on Abel's tongue—
for his reign has just begun.

Clocks

My mother has so many clocks
the ticking sounds
like a tree full of birds,
and the birds sound like her neighbors:
Sylvia, the rabbi's mother;

Sarah, who shares her newspaper;
and Dorothy, who still drives,
but only to the synagogue
for free lunches. All day
voices float through her walls

like dust motes glittering
in a ray of sunshine. Doris
babbles on the phone to her daughter.
Charley, the maintenance man,
bellows hello and blusters

into another apartment, toolbox
clanking, and the old lady
next door talks to her TV.
My mother closes her eyes and waits
for the dizziness to pass, but it doesn't

and as she sways over the carpet
in her small apartment, she holds on
to the corner of the table, the back
of a chair, the wall—
her fingers leaving dark

smudges on the freckled surface.
By dinnertime the ticking's
so loud the voices fall
into silence. Small birds
drop from the trees, their bodies

stuck in the tarry pavement,
and the congregation on the rooftop
across the parking lot gathers
its feathers and vanishes
into the foamy black air.

Outside

When we brought her outside into the sun
and showed her the crocuses,
the violets opening their mouths
to the light, the twiggy
saplings with white fuzz,
she remembered how the locusts teemed
on the branches above her and the men came
and went like fat birds, how she broke
a heel on the high curb
on Euclid Avenue and fell,
tearing the skin from her knees
and ruining her new outfit.

Then after she praised the "pretty" sycamores,
the smell of cedar, the tart
odors rising from the earth,
she remembered the dust on an eyelid,
the flimsy gown, the frail
body in the mirror, its show
of brittle bones, the white
room where she lay for days,
where her mother leaned
over and pressed a fleshy
palm to her forehead
and breathed into her mouth and nostrils,
and she wanted to wake
from death one more time.

Later, in the sweltering heat,
gnats swarmed over
the pavement and her head sagged
toward her chest as though the body
were a tulip closing in shadows.

Nuclear Bomb Drill

At 1:59 p.m. Miss Rudloaf
got up from her desk and smoothed
the wrinkles from her calf-length
blue dress. She hung a thin
white cardigan over her shoulders,
then with a flick of the wrist, signaled
us to stand in the aisles. As she placed
a piece of chalk in the grooved
holder attached to the board,
the alert sounded, and her red
cheeks grew redder. "Line up,"
she commanded, "and no talking."
By the window, I cupped my ears
and watched the raindrops slide
from the slick surfaces of leaves
and the pigeons waddling across the lawn
until Peggy Kelly, a slender girl
with freckles, took my hand.
We went in pairs down
the long corridor, heels
clacking against linoleum. On the steps,
holding the rail, I leaned close
and could smell her sugary breath
and clean reddish hair.
Behind Miss Rudloaf, we hurried
down three flights of steps,
past the locked door to
the teachers' lounge, past
the furnace room exhaling
its hot oily breath,
past the Lost and Found—
filled with gloves, stocking
caps and Cracker Jack rings—
into the narrow passage that led
to the lower playroom, a room
with no windows. She held open
the door and ushered us in,
repeating the instruction,
"Go to the space near post 1."
The cement was cool on my face

and hands and I stared at the blushed
pink skin peeking out from the space
between Peggy's white shirt and kilt.
As the voice of the principal rasped
over the loudspeaker, like a harsh
wind passing over our bodies,
I let my fingers inch
over the cement toward her bare
skin. When I touched her,
she fidgeted and giggled as if tickled
and turned toward me. In an instant
Miss Rudloaf stood over us in clunky
black pumps. "If you don't
watch it, you'll stay after school
for an entire week," she shouted
and then retreated to her position,
holding knees close together
and lowering herself to the floor.
I didn't want to be kicked out
of the nuclear bomb drill
so I closed my eyes and rehearsed
my final moment on earth
in silence, and my hand reached out
to find Peggy, but this time
she didn't laugh or move.

Sunday School
The Plagues

As the fat rabbi out front
of Shaare Emeth says a prayer
to his black Cadillac, parked in a
no parking zone,
as the old ladies totter toward
the mahjong tables at Golden Fry,
I peek through my folded hands
in the temple, and serpents hiss
and go to war on the cement floor,
and the frogs teem on the tables, and
locusts swarm the foliage
until everything is bare as the white
tablecloth on which the bread is cut,
and the rabbi beats his drum
and the gowns of the singers drop
to the floor, and red wine
overflows the silver cups
as the Egyptian Bride unwraps
her layers of silk, as I taste
the crumbs of honey cake
on Sally's Abrams' warm lips,
as the Red Sea parts again
and the gowns rise like plagues,
as wind blows over the desert,
as white sand glistens on the table,
as Moses bears the scroll
of the Torah on his shoulders, cutting
through the sea, and the soldiers
drown in his wake and the darkness
is so thick we are pressed into it,
as the frogs bring wisdom to our windows,
as the flies learn to love us, as the
nails soften in the wood
and fish flit through water,
as the old women at Golden Fry
lean over the mahjong tiles,
ready to go down, as Pharaoh's
heart hardens again
and Moses pronounces the last
plague, and the black Cadillac
pulls away from the curb.

Sunday

for the uncles

On Sunday you slap your palms
on the table and roll your heads
and lift your eyes to the dust
floating down from the dirty stars.
On Sunday you recall the tailors
clustered in a small room,
yards of yellow tape
measures, thumbs pressing tape
from cuff to crotch,
mouths full of bright
pins. On Sunday
you stretch and shift and yawn and
fart and let out the bad,
air into the rooms where your daughters
pick up the dirty dishes
and wrinkle their noses. On
Sunday you stare into the eyes
of the wind and touch
the crumbled lips of roses,
the speckled blue eggs
cracked on the pavement, the throbbing
nests that tumble from branches,
as squirrels rob the trees blind,
as you remember the ruined dreams
of your fathers, the tiny spiders
attaching themselves to flesh,
the bell shattering over the steep hillsides,
moths clustered in the forest,
the nimbus of breath fading.
And your bodies turn
to globes of pain, sugar
burning your bitter tongues.

Call from Little Rock

When my bus ticket to Portland vanished,
I wound up in Little Rock, where steam rose
from the gutters and my sandals stuck
to the gooey asphalt. While I slept

someone stuck a needle in my arm—my body
unwound over the buggy water,
spinning away from its center
until nothing was left of me but a spool, white

and shiny plastic. On the seventh day
I woke in the chew tank with thirty others,
my mouth so dry I could barely talk
and water sat on my tongue like a lozenge.

I forgot about seeing my grandmother,
stuck in a nursing home near Scarsdale.
I forgot about talking to my kid,
long-legged and beautiful.

I forgot about her mother and the money I owed them.
For weeks I assembled toys and handed out
bright sticky flags on a street corner
and listened to coins clink in my paper cup

while my brothers smoked crack in the alley.
All afternoon I smelled lollipops and roasted peanuts,
and colorful balloons rose in the air.
At night in the Mission I thought about my lover—

a junkie with a nest of red hair and beautiful blue eyes,
who cleaned out my apartment and stole my truck—
and wondered what I'd done wrong.
The bare bulbs blinked off. My brothers drummed

the walls with yellowed palms.
When I couldn't remember her face—now an iridescent
glow in the tattered sky of my memory—
I locked myself in this phone booth and called you collect.

Summer of '69

That summer the tired bells
cracked, and even shaded
windows sweated out the day.

Julie, Stumper, Jimmy,
Gardner and I
sat in a field at SIU,
500 yards from the stage
where Bob Dylan played
a 5-song set with The Band,
opening with "I Ain't Got
No Home in This World Anymore."
And before the concert was over, Stumper
did a dance that made everyone laugh,
and Julie passed out in the weeds.

That summer we licked blotter paper
and went to the park with our shirts
off, quacking like ducks
and splashing the filthy water,
where used rubbers, dirty syringes,
cigarette butts and beer cans floated.
When Julie took off her top to sunbathe,
young mothers grabbed their infants
as they shouted curses and ran from us.

That summer, in his parents'
house, Gardner dissolved
crystal meth in boiling
water, scorching the bottom
of his mother's spoon with the flame
of a butane lighter. He tapped out
the air bubbles and squeezed
the plunger into my arm. And one night
I woke in a hospital gown,
my face yellowed like an old bruise.

That summer Jimmy took
a bad hit and died
with a needle in his arm. Vicki
popped too many pills
and downed half a bottle
of red wine, dancing naked
in Wag's apartment until she
collapsed on the scuffed wood floor.
By the time anyone noticed,
it was too late to wake her.
And Paul, drunk on bourbon
and stoned on Seconals, swerved
his 'Vette into a concrete divider
and died on Highway 40.

That summer we waited
for the long days to end,
for night to begin, but horseflies
clustered in the dewy closets,
and the moon spun its terrible
tale to the broken nests
and the quiet feathers falling
for miles smothered
the dark fires of the street.

Heat

Below our window
men slouched farther
into the benches, walleyed
from staring into bright windows.
The merchants called it a day
and pushed their tables back
inside and rolled up striped canopies.

Under the marquee at the Tivoli
a truck sputtered and collapsed on its wheels.
Yellow flowers swooned in planters.
Spiders clung to webs
above the simmering tar,
and wasps whispered in their paper nest
under the eaves.

We lay back down,
waiting for the heat to break,
waiting for night.

In the damp sheets, you dreamed
you were a cool rain
dowsing the branches of the sycamores,
and I was a big wind in blue shoes,
kicking up puddles.

The moon sweltered, dripping
wax down our windows.
Even the darkness failed us.

The Long Heat Wave

for Gerald Stern
Give me back the long heat wave, the sweat dripping
from eyelashes, the stained blouses, the black windows,
the spiders dangling from their silver bridges,
the wasps lighting on the branches of the cedar bushes
as they waited for me to make a dash for the screen door.
Give me back Herman Meltzer, our upstairs neighbor,
who forged his last check with a flourish before the police
took him away in his checked pajamas, handcuffed.
Give me back Hanna Gorelick in her red satin robe,
her hair in rollers; and Cathy Cowser naked in front of the
            window;
and "A Day in the Life" with its scratches and pops,
John Lennon singing "I read the news today, oh boy . . .";
and my thick brown hair—every morning
I brushed it down so hard my scalp stung, but the curls
sprung up before I left the bathroom mirror;
and my father warning the butcher at Sherman's Deli
not to trim off too much fat from the corned beef.
And give me back Barbie Silverman's long smooth legs
in her black short shorts, the Santa Maria rising from
the bottom of the river, the goddess undressing in the eye of
            the Arch
as the rabbis chanted to the brown muddy water.
Give me back the blue butterflies streaming
through the emptiness above the tall white sycamores,
the speckled blackbirds shitting on the Handshears'
new Oldsmobile, no matter where they parked.
Give me back my mother balancing her checkbook at the
            kitchen table—
"Everyone in Israel is beautiful," she says; and
my father in his shorts, thumbing through
a thumb-size version of *The New Testament* and
marking in red the passages he would use to make his sales
            pitch to the goyim,

raising his fist to the TV tube every time he hears
another special report—"But is it good for the Jews?"—
and my sister with her thick black hair,
waiting by the silent phone for a date to call.
Give me back the burning red coils in the sky, the plague
        of locusts,
God railing into the wind, the dark news that floats through
        the windows,
the spark of light at the beginning of our world.

New Car

His eyes silvery like Kennedy
half-dollars, my father guns
the engine of a new navy blue
Riviera with hidden headlamps
while I crawl over the backseat,
touching the velvety upholstery,
the silver ashtray,
the automatic window buttons.
But my mother stands on the sidewalk
away from the open door,
"How can we afford this?"

Gnats spin in the hot air
and a few birds work the lawns
and the sun rides its rim
of red dust. When at last she gets in,
running her fingers over the dash
my father twists the air-conditioning
knob to high, and cold
air blows into the back
and the smell of formaldehyde
rises from the warm carpet.

"How can you make a buck,"
he asks, "without a car?"
and takes us for a spin,
easing over the speed bumps
on Carswold, coasting past
the huge homes of rich people,
coasting under the tall sycamores
until he veers onto the entrance ramp
of Highway 40 and opens it up,

flooring the gas pedal,
and we're doing a hundred m.p.h.
in seconds. "That's power," he shouts.

"Slow up," my mother says,
"What's the matter with you?"
but he's caught up in the joy of speed,
shooting past the other cars,
into sheets of glaring light.
I squint, but still can't
see where the road is going.
Space curves with us
as the needle climbs to 115.
"Stop, Paul," my mother shouts

and I push back against the seat
bracing my feet against the floor,
the sudden field tipping
into shadow. In a blink
some locusts crack on the windshield
and a siren breaks through the sound
of wind, and my father stares
into the rearview at the flashing
red, easing his foot
down on the power brake.

The Twist

When Miss Wait pulled out
a nubby white towel
and wrapped it around her bony hips
and swiveled them side to side,
we all laughed at how ridiculous
she looked, dancing like a teenager
on *American Bandstand*. The climbing ropes
dropped from the rafters, the loose
strands on their knotted ends
tickling the gray wrestling mats.
In his penguin shirt Mr. Burdick,
who called Dale Dickler "Lard
Butt" and me "Jew Boy,"
blew Miss Wait a kiss
and went to his office behind the caged
window to scribble on papers
or clean up his shelves. At least
until tomorrow we wouldn't hear him
tell us what losers we were,
nor would we have to pick sides
for football or soccer.
While Chubby Checker sang
about walking twenty miles
to see his lover, Miss Wait's
bright red lips, thin
as scars, spread into a smile
and she extended her hand to all of us.
Under the bright gym lights
we twisted closer and closer
pumping our arms and rolling
our hips at a furious pitch
until we laughed so hard we forgot
this was gym class—no one
left out or unchosen.

Out of Reach

Beyond us the fox gloats
in the gloaming, his mouth full
of bloody feathers and the chickens
clamor for justice—a posse of voices—

until shots ring out. Dipping his antlers
the moose robs the broken ash,
then licks up salt at the
rutted edge of the highway.

Darkness coming on, the brook
rides past the Abenaki
burial ground, past the ancient
rocks where I watched a spotted

hawk dive into the woods,
where I lay down
and felt the knuckled memories
drumming inside the hardened earth.

Now a flame hisses in the white globes
strung in the pines. In the ravine
coyotes yip around a glowing carcass
and a dog howls tethered to a wire.

As frayed nests fall, as moths
flatten their wings and disappear,
the owl's jewels glint just out of
reach in the dark above the beams.

Memorial

It's nice to remember the houses
floating on water. It's nice
to stand on shore and sing
a hymn of praise
while candles burn
in the windows.
It's nice to dream the loaves
rising in ovens
and the floors dusted with flour,
the women with beautiful
hair falling like cities
into darkness, the long
nights of love. It's nice to pretend
we could have saved them.
It's nice to say a few
words as spring turns to fall,
as fall turns to winter, and winter to spring.
It's nice to return again
and stare at the stars
so bright and forgettable.
It's nice to remember laughter
spilling into the wind,
roses sprouting from their fleshy mouths
as children fall down
and down into the dirt.
It's nice to remember the voices
calling for you, calling
back the curtains, calling
through the long sleeves, the hollow places.
It's nice to remember the feast
of speckled blackbirds
huddled on the rims
of roofs, the stars
drawn in ash on the doorways,
the lament of uncles—
the long dance that kicked
up the dust and crinkled leaves,
the bodies waiting to burn,
the ash drifting on water.

FOUR

Hymn to Your Tongue

I come back to your tongue
dreaming in seven languages,
in a flurry of feathers,
in a swarm of white moths,
in a blue fog over three
bridges, your tongue
dreaming in seven countries
where trails clamber up through
high rocks, fleshy
hearts, clusters of ferns,
where dizzy orange salamanders
search for the river, where wolf
spiders cling to speckled eggs,
floating down from the wet
heavens, where kings reign
over courts of wildflowers, over plump
pods, over spores
that glitter in the rusty rays.
I come back to your tongue
singing in flight, circling
the twiggy nest, your tongue
swimming through creamy combers,
humming in the velvet hive,
your tongue lingering in the salty heat,
the sultry hair, rolling over
beaded abacuses, parting the
fuzzy skirts of purple cabbages, your tongue
tasting the glorious yoke, the sweet
fire, the burning chasm.

Salt House

And in bright excellence adorned, crested
With every prodigal, familiar fire
                              —Wallace Stevens
Throughout winter orange flies
embedded themselves in the wood
and smoldered. Jill crayoned
green circles on manila
paper poking each
one with angry dots.
"Let her be," you said.

I lay down for a rest
but the dotted mice got inside,
scratching at the walls. The doves
plucked their string, which vibrated
its one tiresome note over the sand. I waited.
Fat sizzled in the skillet.

Where the rocks were buttered green,
we found rusted barbs
with the memories of fish, their eyes
bulging against the brisk air.
We clambered up the blue dune—up
to our knees in sand, white
crumbs on our lips—only
to return to what we left.

Forgive me for all
the prodigal, familiar fires
that held us in the dappled dark—
a still-born love—as it took
our breath into the foaming flame.

After the Funeral Service

The dog stares at the crumpled
covers, but they don't move.
The yellow light touches
the couch, the table, the wooden
spindles of the chairs
with the same heat.
The fruit basket is empty,
the flowers gone,
trays of cold cuts
emptied into the garbage, set
out on the curb in plump
plastic bags. Crows
still huddle in their dark
suits. They scribble notes
and seal envelopes.
Thousands of balloons fly
into the air. The Ferris wheel
circles against blue sky—
so many bright faces
drinking in sun.

Beam

As I drove home from the hospital,
where my mother lay
in the ICU, a fox
lunged into the beam of my headlights.

I got out to look for her,
and just when I thought
she was gone, she put her paws
on the stone ledge on the slope
of a lawn and stared back at me,
her large ears twitching
as if trying to flick off a fly.

Afraid the fox might bolt
if I took a step, I remained
where I was in the road.

Between us, gnats swarmed
above the cedar bushes and dusk
dwindled to a single gold
coin, glittering a moment, then gone.

After the Storm

I swept the blue shells
that cracked on the cement and three
lifeless fetuses–pink
and rubbery—into a paper bag,
but placed the phoebe's nest
on the ledge, not knowing what
I'd do with it. As I walked out
with the bag in my hand, a cool wind
breathed through the tall pines.
The finches and chickadees still sang
and a hummingbird streaked through
the air, sunlight striking
its iridescent green back.
Around the bend azaleas had thrown
down their purple blossoms
like thick skirts bunched
in the grass. A young woman
hurried by in a gray sweatsuit,
swinging her arms. The sun
disappeared behind thick clouds.
And the houses sitting above the ravine
turned dark. Broken limbs
hung in the trees or lay on the ground,
and I could hear branches snapping.
I passed a mound of mulch
and smelled the manure raked
into the garden. I passed a dead
raccoon crushed into the asphalt.
I passed a yard where the crows
flew up into the birches and cawed out

their warning. I passed a yard where the bear
had been, the pole of the feeder
bent almost in two, ripped
from the ground, seed scattered.
I entered the woods,
stepping over fallen
tree trunks, kicking up
pine needles and cones—
my path winding and twisting
down to the jagged rock
that jutted over the river, where
I crouched and made an offering.

Cassandra

Before Apollo spit
his curse onto my tongue,
I lived without bitterness and fear.

He abandoned me the way
one might abandon
a box of sentimental keepsakes—

carved winged horses,
a ring made of leather,
good luck medallions,

wood dolphins
painted blue and white,
their fins extended like wings.

I remember his sweetness
like strawberries burning,
the blazing wings,

white hooves
pounding the sky
to blue powder.

Taking the South

for Nathan Schwartz

This is the desert our fathers
promised us, the holy rocks,
the eternity of white sand,
the caves full of computers
and explosives, the air germy
with hate. Lying on my belly
I smell the oil oozing from the
body of earth, black fires
burning. When I call out
no one answers. In the fiery
cumulus, angels wring
drops of acid from their shirts.
My eyes burn, and my hand
lobs its grenade, and shards of
metal shower into trenches.
I tighten my mask. It'll be a long
night waiting for the husky
shadows to unsheathe their knives,
repeating their orders,
waiting for the bird on my shoulder
to say its prayer and fly into
the drifts of dust, into the funnel's
drumbeat, the whistling
that kills the voices in our brains.
In my dreams my friends and I shake
and thrust on the dance floor,
and the ladies love us
for our beards, for the touch of our hands,
for the laughter that explodes from our guts,
for the sweet red wine on our lips.

Michal

Bitter were the bees
that clustered above us,
swarming the faces
of the spirits that haunted
my father. And the air
we breathed was bitter.

The old man rose
from the earth feet first
like some hideous baby,
denouncing everything
around him, even the songs of birds—
"False prophets," he called them.

"Don't be misled."
But the young shepherd
smelled sweet like a girl
and his kisses were sweet,
and I loved him for what he was,
not what he would become,

and I held his body against mine
half the night, shielding him,
and I deceived my father with a sheet
and a pillow of goat's hair.
Bitter were the knives glinting in
the sun, shouting down the walls—

and the king danced before the bees—
and bitter, the storm of salt,
the grasshoppers chirring
in the wheat field, mourning
my father, his feet
naked in the dust.

Oenone Settles It with Paris

It's time to put the past
behind us, but where do I go
to forget her long black
hair, her violet eyes,
moist lips whispering
"Paris'll always be mine."

I watched them carry you up
the mountain, winding through
rocks and twisted ferns.
When you were near the top, I
dusted off my vials of tinctures,
jars of crushed herbs and waited.

They set you down
at my feet, and when you rolled off
your bier, unable to stand
and greet me, I knelt,
squeezed your hand and kissed you,
smelled your fetid breath.

I remember how you begged
for your life, promising
to love me forever, how you praised
my eyes, my hair, my breasts, how you said
I was even more beautiful than Helen—
your last lie.

Goodbye

We're leaning on the railing,
watching the gulls float
and the jellyfish swell
into pink balloons.

It's nice to be together again.
You point to the island
in the distance and wave
as though you had spotted a friend.

Everything is so blue,
so clear there is no
need for fear,
and nothing can come between us.

The barge sputters on.
The gulls take off
and wheel above us.
For one brief moment,

the sun is blinding
and the polished horizon blurs.
The island vanishes.
I say goodbye once more.

Even the water disappears,
though the barge
rides out
the choppy waves.

Two Women

When Leah sneaks in late at night,
she brings almonds and figs,
a taste of stolen wine.

She tells me
what we could make together
if I would forget her sister.

When I touch her
and lick the cloud from her body,
she quivers like a sky of bright seeds.

"Forget my sister," she repeats
but when the moon lights
her twelve candles,

it is Rachel
who sits on my thighs,
who bites my lips and laughs,

who seizes me with her arms and legs,
her burning prophecy,
Rachel, whose hair is darker than darkness.

The Promised Land

after Amir Gilboa

When I found my father
after so many years of wandering
and showed him the right way to go
he put his arm around my shoulder
and called me "son."

Crows flew up,
announcing my triumph to the hazy sky.
My lovers arose
from their blankets and saluted me.

Shelley, my first love, was there, recalling
our night in the weeds, among the crickets.
And there was Mick from Granite City,
reciting my list of failures
and pining for the man
who dumped her for another.

And there was beautiful Sarah,
who cut off her long black hair
and wouldn't get out of bed for weeks.
And Jennifer with her pillowy thighs,
who left me with a little dust
in my hands and some change
shining on the sill.

I unfolded the map,
drawing stars on our path in charcoal.
"You're such a boy," he said
and pointed the way back,
where she who loved me
still waited.

Making It to Tina Turner

I stole three airline bottles
of Johnny Walker Red
from my father's liquor cabinet
and drank them with Annie Storm
under the trestle where peepers croaked
and newts glowed orange
crawling away from the river.
"You think we can get in?"
"I know it," she said
and took my hand and led me
through the cattails and tall weeds
to a narrow alley
lit by a single lamp
and the glitter of broken bottles.
We hid behind some garbage cans
and waited for our chance
while the guy at the door, a box
of cigarettes rolled up in his sleeve,
leaned against the brick wall
and took a long last drag,
then flicked the butt into the gravel.
"Be patient," she whispered,
touching her fingers to her soft lips.
Less than ten feet away,
we could hear Tina Turner
wailing the close of "Proud Mary,"
her voice screaming toward the stars.
When the bouncer went to take
a piss behind a boarded up building,
we made a dash for the door,
but another man, large
and beefy, stepped out in front of us.
For a moment he held us there,
blocking our path, but as Ike's

long pearly fingers
stroked the strings of his electric
guitar and Tina Turner
whispered into the mike, "Fool
in Love," the man grinned down at us,
stepped out of the way,
and we slipped into the hot, sticky
darkness for the final song.

Hunting with My Father

Rabbit carcasses hang
from branches—too many
to count—their tender bodies
glowing like fat pink
fireflies. My father slides
his blade over my index finger,
opens a seam in the flesh.
"That's how sharp." I squeeze it
to shut off the blood.

Tree frogs clamor,
and an owl hoots. In the gully
coyotes yip and howl
circling their prey under the milky
birches. I smell the blood
combed through my father's thinning
brown hair, flecked
with red. He tells me to
watch closely, then skins

another rabbit. In the distance
the late train to Davenport
smokes over the rails
and a car patches out on Route 9.
Every fall my father
travels north to Canada
to hunt moose, elk, deer
and wolves, but now he's content
to be here, crouched in the forest.

Even though it is night,
he squints his left eye,
aims his rifle as though sighting
a shape bunched in the tall,
wet grass. I sharpen
the knife against stone
until sparks shower his shoes,
and the blade lights a path
through the guts of rabbits.

The Waiting Room at St. Mary's Hospital

They littered the tables and floors
with empty donut boxes,
crushed soda cans,
plastic cups, half-eaten
sandwiches and crumpled greasy
papers. Children rampaged
through the room, jumping off
tables and sprawling out
on the floor.

My mother was dying,
so I sat alone, but one
kid kept pushing
his crayon drawings in my face.
Leaning against a wall, the father
opened his palms and held them
out as if testing the air
for rain. "Josh's in fifth
grade," the mother told me.
"He loves art. Shelly's in
third—the twins are in first."
Then her cell phone rang.

The lights flickered. Across the hall,
those who were dying slept fitfully.
I prayed for a little peace.
As the kids hurled themselves
into the open couch, laughing
and screaming, I pointed my index
finger, cocked my thumb,
then picked them off, one by one.

Crows

You came with your dark hats,
fringed shawls, gifts—
armloads of flowers and grief.

You came with twigs,
muddy houses, ashes
smeared on your cheeks.

You came with your broken clocks,
loud warnings. You came
with your wisdom,

but your wisdom was air.
You came with your umbrellas open
despite the sun,

and the sun shone in the feathers
of your wings held close
to your bodies. You came with your offering,

the corpses of mice and birds,
bundles of bones,
and the bones were bloody,

and bloody were your beaks
and talons ticking
the long black table.

Notes

"The Golem in the Suburbs" uses imaginary facts from *The Book of Imaginary Beings* by Jorge Luis Borges.

"The Surviving Angel" was inspired by Rafael Alberti's angel poems, translated by Mark Strand.

"The Mournful Dress" picks up a phrase or two from a poem by the Mexican poet Ramón López Velarde, translated by Margaret Sayers Peden.

"Birthday" begins with a line from an early Tennyson poem.

"The Long Heat Wave" is indebted to Philip Levine's poem "You Can Have It."

The poem "Memorial" owes a great deal to Gerald Stern's powerful book *Paradise Poems*.

2004
Freeways and Aqueducts, James Harms
Tristimania, Mary Ruefle
Prague Winter, Richard Katrovas
Venus Examines Her Breast, Maureen Seaton
Trains in Winter, Jay Meek
The Women Who Loved Elvis All Their Lives, Fleda Brown
The Chronic Liar Buys a Canary, Elizabeth Edwards
Various Orbits, Thom Ward

2005
Laws of My Nature, Margot Schilpp
Things I Can't Tell You, Michael Dennis Browne
Renovation, Jeffrey Thomson
Sleeping Woman, Herbert Scott
Blindsight, Carol Hamilton
Fallen from a Chariot, Kevin Prufer
Needlegrass, Dennis Sampson
Bent to the Earth, Blas Manuel De Luna

2006
Burn the Field, Amy Beeder
Dog Star Delicatessen: New and Selected Poems 1979-2006,
        Mekeel McBride
The Sadness of Others, Hayan Charara
A Grammar to Waking, Nancy Eimers
Shinemaster, Michael McFee
Eastern Mountain Time, Joyce Peseroff
Dragging the Lake, Robert Thomas

2007
So I Will Till the Ground, Gregory Djanikian
Trick Pear, Suzanne Cleary
Indeed I Was Pleased With the World, Mary Ruefle
The Situation, John Skoyles
One Season Behind, Sarah Rosenblatt
The Playhouse Near Dark, Elizabeth Holmes
Drift and Pulse, Kathleen Halme
Black Threads, Jeff Friedman
On the Vanishing of Large Creatures, Susan Hutton